GORDON PARKS
NO EXCUSES

GORDON PARKS
NO EXCUSES

TEXT BY: ANN PARR
PHOTOGRAPHS BY: GORDON PARKS

ILLUSTRATIONS BY: KATHRYN BREIDENTHAL

Kathryn Breidenthal

PELICAN PUBLISHING COMPANY
Gretna 2006

*Heartfelt thanks to Gordon Parks for his time, his art, and especial-
ly his friendship; my Vermont College advisors and classmates for
suggesting the best words; my husband, Jack, for our team effort
as we share the journey; and our daughters, Cheri and Cynda, for
their photographic advice and expertise*

*The word "Pelican" and the depiction of a pelican are
trademarks of Pelican Publishing Company, Inc., and are
registered in the U.S. Patent and Trademark Office.*

Library of Congress Cataloging-in-Publication Data

Parr, Ann.
   Gordon Parks : no excuses / by Ann Parr ; photographs by Gordon
Parks.
      p. cm.
   ISBN-13: 978-1-58980-411-1 (hardcover : alk. paper)
   1. Parks, Gordon, 1912- 2. African American photographers--
Biography--Juvenile literature. 3. Photographers--United States--
Biography--Juvenile literature. I. Parks, Gordon, 1912- II. Title.
   TR140.P35P3564 2006
   770.92--dc22

                                        2005034797

*Art credits: Pages 1, 29 by Ann Parr; pages 2, 3 courtesy Don
Miller, Historical Fort Scott; pages 8, 16, 17, 24 courtesy Getty
Images; page 12 courtesy Minnesota Historical Society*

Printed in China
Published by Pelican Publishing Company, Inc.
1000 Burmaster Street, Gretna, Louisiana 70053

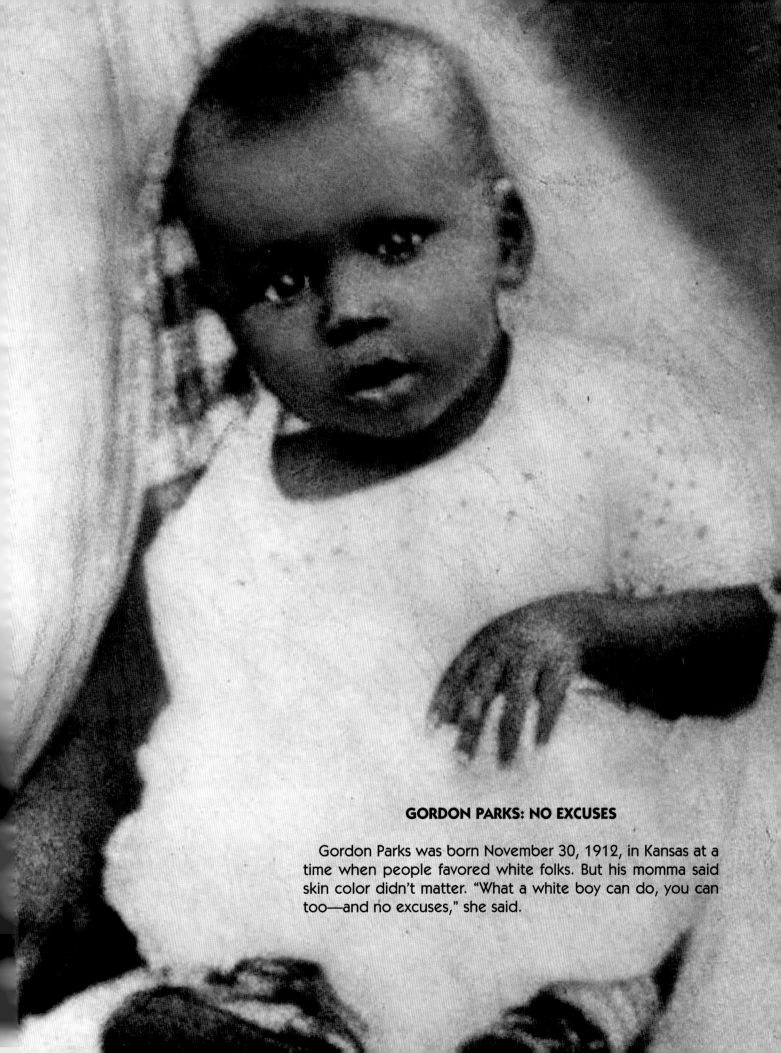

GORDON PARKS: NO EXCUSES

Gordon Parks was born November 30, 1912, in Kansas at a time when people favored white folks. But his momma said skin color didn't matter. "What a white boy can do, you can too—and no excuses," she said.

Gordon's momma died when he was sixteen. He missed Momma terribly when he moved to Minnesota.

Gordon searched for work to buy a little food and a place to sleep. Few people would hire a black boy. Gordon kept looking.

At last, Gordon found work as a waiter on the Northern Pacific Railroad. One day he borrowed a passenger's *Life* magazine.

Photographs of poor families disheartened him, and pictures of Paris fashions stirred his curiosity. Sometime later, Gordon noticed the word *LIFE* on a passenger's camera bag. He asked the photographer, Mr. Capa, about his job. Gordon wondered if he, too, could become a photographer for *Life,* a world-famous magazine.

Gordon began to study more pictures, visit art museums in Chicago, and buy books to learn about photographing light and dark and shadows.

He recalled Momma's words. "What a white boy can do, you can too—no excuses."

Gordon bought a camera and started taking pictures.
"You've got a good eye," the camera-shop clerk told Gordon.
"Keep that up and we'll offer you an exhibit."

Before long, the Kodak camera shop in St. Paul, Minnesota, displayed Gordon's pictures in their front window: seagulls, old men, signs, clouds, children, sand dunes, and boat docks. Gordon paced back and forth, pretending he was a world-famous photographer.

In downtown St. Paul, Gordon visited department stores, asking owners if he could photograph their goods and models. Some laughed at him. Others called him names. "Go away, black man," they chided.

But storeowner Madeline Murphy said, "I'll give you a chance. Can you be here tomorrow evening?"

The next evening at Murphy's fashion store, Gordon arranged furniture and lights and drapes to photograph models wearing lovely gowns.

"How beautiful!" Mrs. Murphy exclaimed. She loved the way Gordon's style of contrasts and shadows showed off her models and clothing. "If you can do pictures like that, I want more."

Gordon also photographed Chicago's poor living in cardboard boxes and New York's children begging for food. These pictures helped him win an award to study with famous photographers in Washington, D.C.

Finally, twelve years later, he headed for *Life* magazine.

Gordon tiptoed past the secretary into *Life* magazine's New York office. *Life* had never hired a black photographer before. Momma would have said, "That's no excuse."

He slipped into the picture editor's office.

Wilson Hicks jerked up his head. "How'd you get in here?"

"Just walked in," Gordon said.

"Then you can turn around and walk out."

"Won't you take a quick look at my work first?" Gordon asked.

Mr. Hicks studied Gordon's photographs. He raised his eyebrows, peered over his glasses at Gordon, and studied them some more. "What do you want to photograph?" he asked.

Gordon had to think fast. He remembered growing up poor, being called names, and later living in a rat-infested New York boardinghouse. "I want to photograph gang wars in Harlem," he said. Harlem is a neighborhood in New York.

"That's dangerous," Mr. Hicks said. "Gangs are violent."

Gordon's heart sank. He wished he'd given a better answer.

"All I can give you is two hundred dollars," Mr. Hicks said.

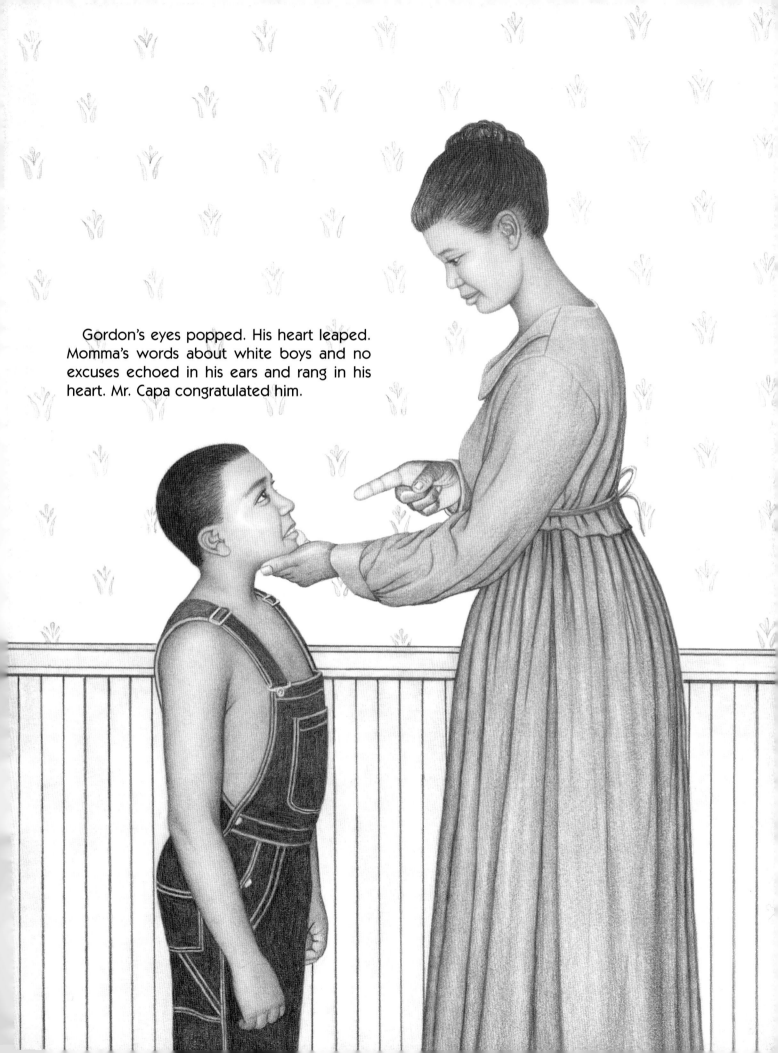

Gordon's eyes popped. His heart leaped. Momma's words about white boys and no excuses echoed in his ears and rang in his heart. Mr. Capa congratulated him.

Gordon set out to find Harlem's most feared gang leader, Red Jackson. But Red said his "Midtowners" would not want their story to be in a world-famous magazine.

"They will if they see your picture," Gordon replied.
Red brightened. "Wait," he said. "I'll ask my warlords."

Red's story and pictures appeared in *Life* on November 1, 1948. Wilson Hicks liked the story. So did Henry Luce, *Life*'s owner.

Gordon's telephone rang. "Henry wants you to photograph fashions in Paris," Wilson said.

Gordon danced a jig to celebrate.

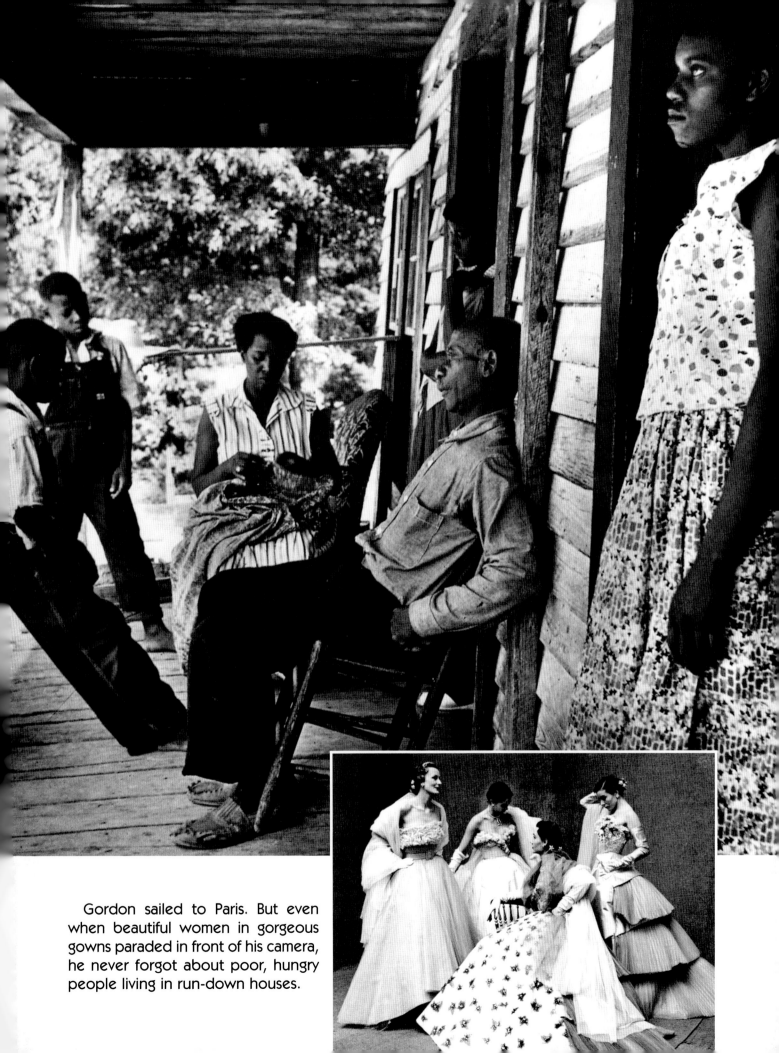

Gordon sailed to Paris. But even when beautiful women in gorgeous gowns paraded in front of his camera, he never forgot about poor, hungry people living in run-down houses.

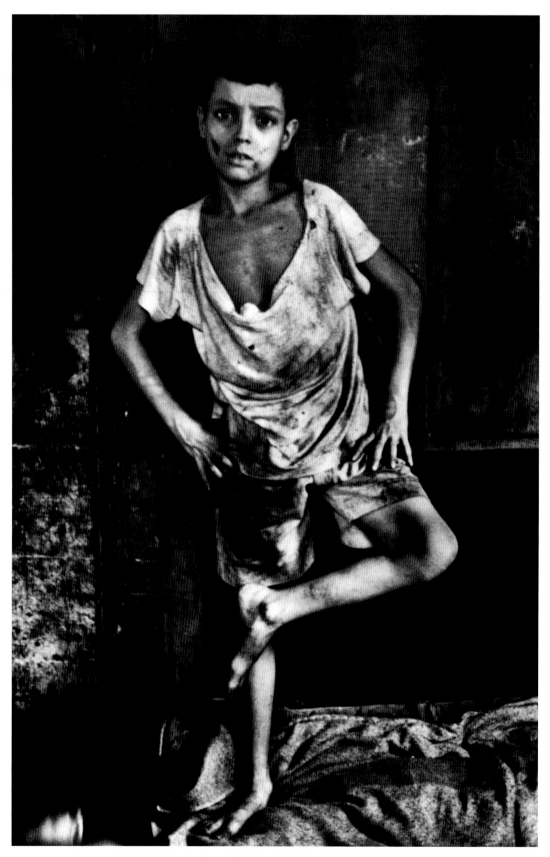

Gordon wrote about the ravaged Catacumba slums on the hillsides above Rio de Janeiro, Brazil. His photographs of Flavio da Silva's struggle to keep his family of ten alive showed Latin America's poverty to the world.

During the 1960s, Gordon went where white photographers were not welcome to report on the Civil Rights movement. He wrote about Malcolm X's Black Muslims, Stokely Carmichael's Black Power movement, and Martin Luther King Jr.'s funeral.

Gordon told the story of Bessie Fontenelle. She told him
there was no job for her husband, no heat or electricity in
their apartment, and no food for her children.

Gordon also taught himself to paint, make movies, and compose music. He wrote twenty-four books, including *The Learning Tree* and *A Hungry Heart*. And he stayed with *Life* for twenty-five years. He proved that what a white boy could do, he could too—with no excuses.

Whenever Gordon thought about his momma and how her wisdom had helped him overcome so many obstacles . . .

he would open his arms wide, look toward the clouds, and whisper . . .

"Thank you, Momma."